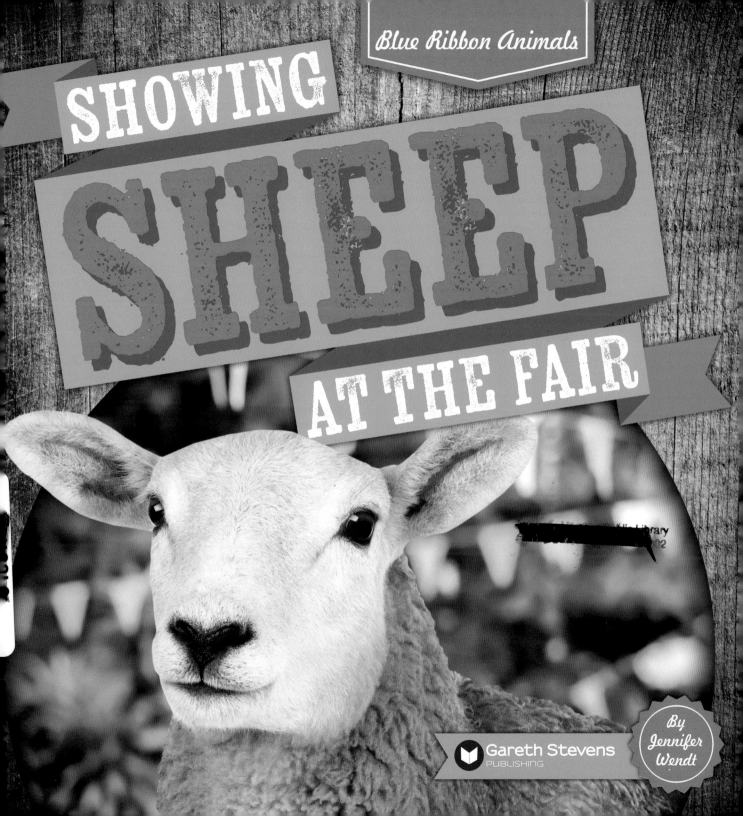

Blue Ribbon Animals

# SHOWING SHEEP AT THE FAIR

Gareth Stevens
PUBLISHING

By Jennifer Wendt

Please visit our website, www.garethstevens.com. For a free color catalog of all our high-quality books, call toll free 1-800-542-2595 or fax 1-877-542-2596.

Library of Congress Cataloging-in-Publication Data

Names: Wendt, Jennifer, author.
Title: Showing sheep at the fair / Jennifer Wendt.
Description: New York : Gareth Stevens Publishing, [2019] | Series: Blue ribbon animals | Includes index.
Identifiers: LCCN 2018031029| ISBN 9781538229323 (library bound) | ISBN 9781538232941 (paperback) | ISBN 9781538232958 (6 pack)
Subjects: LCSH: Sheep--Showing--Juvenile literature. | Livestock exhibitions--Juvenile literature.
Classification: LCC SF374 .W46 2019 | DDC 636.3/1--dc23
LC record available at https://lccn.loc.gov/2018031029

First Edition

Published in 2019 by
**Gareth Stevens Publishing**
111 East 14th Street, Suite 349
New York, NY 10003

Designer: Katelyn E. Reynolds
Editor: Emily Mahoney

Photo credits: Cover, p. 1 (sheep) Eric Isselee/Shutterstock.com; cover, p. 1 (background photo) chainarong06/Shutterstock.com; cover, p. 1 (blue banner) Kmannn/Shutterstock.com; cover, pp. 1-24 (wood texture) Flas100/Shutterstock.com; pp. 2-24 (paper) Peter Kotoff/Shutterstock.com; p. 5 © iStockphoto.com/Maisna; p. 7 (Dorset) Dick Kenny/Shutterstock.com; p. 7 (Hampshire) travelfoto/Shutterstock.com; p. 7 (Rambouillet) Stephen Hilger/Bloomberg via Getty Images; p. 7 (Suffolk) Pyty/Shutterstock.com; p. 9 hans engbers/Shutterstock.com; p. 11 jaxl0289/Shutterstock.com; p. 12 Richard Thornton/Shutterstock.com; p. 13 Spencer Platt/Getty Images News/Getty Images; p. 15 Ceri Breeze/Shutterstock.com; p. 17 © iStockphoto.com/Jill_InspiredByDesign; pp. 19, 20 © iStockphoto.com/BrandyTaylor; p. 21 Pixels2u/Shutterstock.com.

Printed in the United States of America

CPSIA compliance information: Batch #CW19GS: For further information contact Gareth Stevens, New York, New York at 1-800-542-2595.

# CONTENTS

*Words in the glossary appear in **bold** type the first time they are used in the text.*

# HAVING FUN AT THE FAIR

Going to the fair is exciting! When you go, be sure to visit the animal barns. Kids just like you win blue ribbons by showing their animals at the fair. Some show cows or horses, and some show sheep!

Raising sheep to show at the fair takes a lot of hard work, but it can be a lot of fun, and you'll learn a lot along the way! Read on to learn some basic steps to get your sheep blue-ribbon ready.

## TAKE THE PRIZE!

FEMALE SHEEP ARE CALLED EWES. MALE SHEEP ARE CALLED RAMS. BABY SHEEP ARE CALLED LAMBS. YOU CAN SHOW EWES, LAMBS, AND RAMS AT THE FAIR.

One of the prize-winning sheep at the fair might be yours!

# PICKING A LAMB

Do you have a sheep to show at the fair? You may want to choose a lamb to start with. Lambs are easier to teach than sheep since they're young. Decide which **competition** you're going to show in, and choose a lamb that will be the correct age, weight, and size at the time of the fair.

Your sheep should be friendly so you'll enjoy working with her. Ask your **veterinarian** about the best ways to keep your sheep healthy.

These are just a few of the **breeds** of sheep you can show at the fair.

DORSET

HAMPSHIRE

RAMBOUILLET

SUFFOLK

7

# DAILY CARE

Sheep drink a lot of water—around 2 gallons (7.6 l) each day! Make sure you change your sheep's water every day. Sheep like to eat hay, grass, and grains. You can ask your veterinarian about healthy foods to feed your type of sheep.

Sheep need exercise to stay healthy just like you do. Give them a space where they can run and play to keep them fit and grow into blue-ribbon winners.

## TAKE THE PRIZE!

SHEEP LIVE IN HERDS, WHICH MEANS THEY LIKE TO BE WITH OTHER SHEEP. IF POSSIBLE, KEEP YOUR SHEEP WITH A FEW OF ITS FRIENDS SO IT DOESN'T GET LONELY.

One of the most important things you can do to keep your sheep healthy is make sure it always has a supply of fresh, clean water.

9

# LEADING YOUR LAMB

Start training your sheep to use a **halter** and **lead** when it's a lamb. If you start early, they'll be used to wearing a halter in time for the fair.

Gently put the halter on your lamb's head and leave it there for a bit. Once your lamb is used to the halter, take him for short walks using a lead so he learns to walk with you. This will take time and practice.

## TAKE THE PRIZE!

NEVER LEAVE YOUR SHEEP ALONE WHEN TRAINING IT TO USE A HALTER AND LEAD. YOU WANT MAKE SURE HE'S SAFE!

Training your lamb to use a halter and lead is like training a dog to walk on a leash. You might already know how to do that!

11

# BATH TIME

You'll want to bathe your sheep before the fair. Use livestock soap and be sure to rinse your sheep well. It can take a long time for your sheep to dry, so give yourself enough time before the fair.

Depending on what type of sheep you're showing, you'll either need to **shear** or clip your sheep. You may need to ask an adult for help. Check your sheep's **hooves** to see if they need to be trimmed and remember to clean them too.

Special tools, like the one shown here, can hold your sheep in place while you **groom** her for the fair.

13

# GETTING READY FOR THE FAIR

You'll need a trailer to bring your sheep to the fair. It's a good idea to practice loading your sheep into the trailer before you leave. You may want to play a radio for your sheep so it's familiar with different noises.

Gather all your grooming tools, food, **bedding**, and your show clothes and put them in your show box. When you get to the fair, work with your sheep every day so you're both ready to step into the show-ring.

## TAKE THE PRIZE!

A SHOW BOX IS LIKE A BIG SUITCASE FOR YOUR SHEEP. YOU MIGHT WANT TO KEEP A HALTER, LEAD ROPE, BLANKET, SHOVEL, BUCKET, TOWELS, SOAP, AND CLIPPERS INSIDE FOR THE FAIR.

If you have a long drive to the fair, be sure to stop and check on your sheep in the trailer every once in a while.

LIVE ANIMALS
ANIMAUX VIVANT
LEBENDE TIERE

15

# LET'S GO TO THE FAIR

When you arrive at the fair, sign in and ask where your **pen** is located. Put clean bedding, some food, and plenty of fresh water in your sheep's pen. Be kind and respect your neighbors. Check back often to clean up any messes your sheep makes.

If you have a chance, watch other sheep competitions being judged so you'll be familiar with the what you and your sheep will need to do. Don't forget to have fun and make new friends!

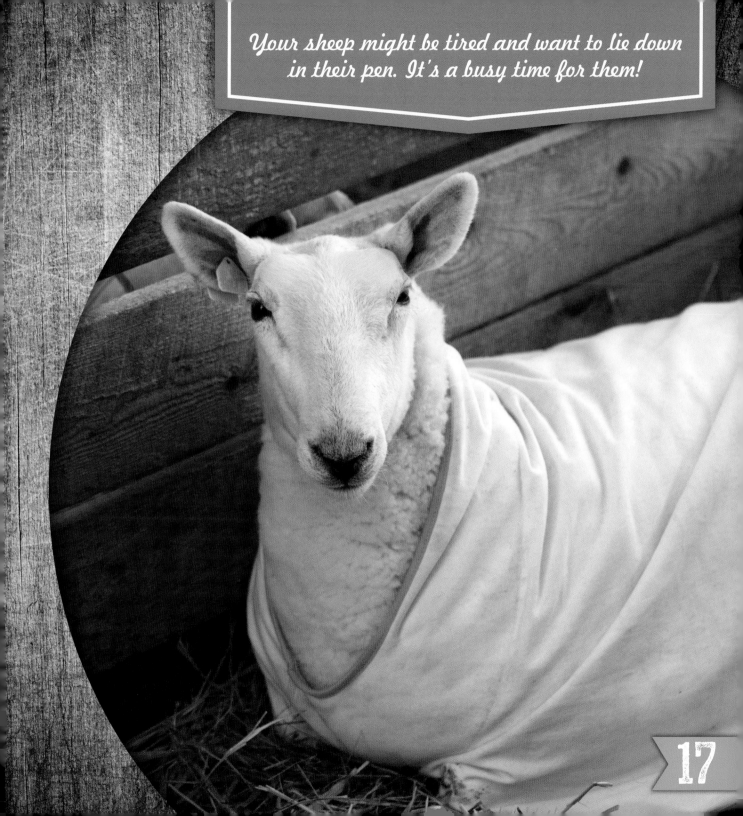

Your sheep might be tired and want to lie down in their pen. It's a busy time for them!

# IN THE SHOW-RING

It's show time! Give your sheep a good rub with a towel to get any bedding off. Clean your sheep's hooves, and wipe off his nose, eyes, and ears. Make sure your clothes are clean, too!

Stay calm in the show-ring and look the judge in the eye when he or she speaks to you. Speak clearly when answering the judge's questions. Be a good sport and cheer on everyone who is showing their sheep. Remember that not everyone can win a blue ribbon.

## TAKE THE PRIZE!

BE READY TO ANSWER THE JUDGE'S QUESTIONS. HE OR SHE MAY ASK THINGS LIKE: WHAT KIND OF SHEEP DO YOU HAVE? HOW MUCH DOES YOUR SHEEP WEIGH? WHAT DO YOU FEED YOUR SHEEP?

Remember to have fun and smile!

19

# TIME TO GO HOME

When it's time to take your sheep home, make sure you leave the pen clean. Pack up your grooming tools, extra food, and bedding. Remember to say thank you to everyone who helped you show your sheep at the fair, and say good-bye to the friends you made!

Whether you won a blue ribbon or not, showing sheep at the fair is fun. Remember what you learned this year and you'll be steps ahead for next year!

With hard work, you and your sheep might earn a blue ribbon!

# GLOSSARY

**bedding:** matter used for an animal's bed, such as straw, newspaper, or wood shavings

**breed:** a group of animals that share features different from other groups of the kind

**competition:** an event in which people try to win

**groom:** to clean

**halter:** a set of straps placed around an animal's head so that the animal can be lead

**hoof:** the hard covering on the foot of an animal such as a horse or sheep. Its plural form is "hooves."

**lead:** a long, thin piece of rope that is used for holding an animal

**pen:** a small enclosed area for farm animals

**shear:** to remove the hair or wool from

**veterinarian:** a doctor who is trained to treat animals

# For More Information

## BOOKS

Esquivel, Rosaura. *Merino Sheep*. New York, NY: PowerKids Press, 2018.

Leighton, Christina. *Sheep*. Minneapolis, MN: Bellwether Media, 2018.

## WEBSITES

### 4-H
4-h.org
4-H gives children a chance to learn new skills through hands-on projects.

### National FFA Organization
www.ffa.org
Future Farmers of America is an education-based organization for students interested in farming.

### Sheep
www.dkfindout.com/us/animals-and-nature/domesticated-animals/sheep/
Fun facts about sheep can be found on this website.

# INDEX